400 AND STILL BURNING

A History of Battle Bonfire and the Battle Bonfire Boyes

M.A. HOAD

400
AND STILL BURNING

A History of Battle Bonfire and The Battle Bonfire Boyes

t₂

Troubador Publishing Ltd
9 De Montfort Mews
Leicester LE1 7FW, UK
Tel: (+44) 116 255 9311 / 9312
Email: books@troubador.co.uk
Web: www.troubador.co.uk/matador

ISBN 978-1905886-951

Typeset in 12pt Stempelgaramond Roman by Troubador Publishing Ltd, Leicester, UK

T2 is an imprint of Troubador Publishing Ltd

CONTENTS

Author's Notes

For those who do not know, the county of Sussex has an odd commitment to the Guy Fawkes celebrations of November the 5th. This created a slight problem when I tried to get this book published because I kept being asked who would be interested in a book about Bonfire Night. Try to explain to people that in Sussex there are nearly thirty bonfire societies and bonfire celebrations in Battle attract around 20,000 people and frankly they do not believe you. Their image of Bonfire Night is a small pile of rubbish in the back garden and a few fireworks for the kids.

I have no allegiance to the BBB so this history is written from an outsider"s view with no bias one way or the other, in fact, there was a period of about ten years during the 80's and 90's that, even though I lived in the town, I did not attend the celebrations. The Battle Bonfire Boyes have had no editorial input to this book; they have only passed on their knowledge and offered lots of help. In fact I am sure there are a few facts and incidents that they wished I had put in and a few they had rather I had left out.

Unfortunately, until recently the Bonfire Boyes kept very little written records of their deeds, or if they did they seem to have been lost. I suppose it would be too much to ask for the society to have its own historian and keep notes of every event. Certainly there are little records of anything pre 1970 and before WW2 little or no records exist except for a few photos and a few memories. As with all histories of local events it is a matter of shifting through what is fact, fiction and myth.

I thank M. J. Hoad for his help, Tom Crawford for his photographs of the 2005 celebration, C. Hoad for his support and everyone who has donated photographs and memories to this project.

I have concentrated the narrative on some of the events that happened in Battle as opposed to Battle Bonfire Boyes visiting other bonfire celebrations around the county.

Any Protestant and Catholic views expressed are not mine or the present Bonfire Society but what seemed apparent at the time they were written.

For ease Battle Bonfire Boyes are generally presented as BBB

FOREWORD

MATT SOUTHAM
CHAIRMAN, BATTLE BONFIRE BOYES

During my years growing up the annual bonfire was always something I looked forward to. Early memories of taking part in the fancy dress competition in the Guide hut are still vivid. I had many costumes, but one that sticks is when I was dressed as Humpty Dumpty. My Father was the wall!

I also used to make a guy that I would proudly take up to the green in the hope that it would get a place at the top of the bonfire. It was during these years that the night before bonfire was comparable to Christmas Eve as far as excitement was concerned. I couldn't get to sleep for memories of past bonfires going through my mind. This still happens to this day and from talking to many other adult members of the society I am not the only one.

Being Chairman during 2005 was a great honour. Not only was it my first year, but it was also the 400th anniversary of the discovery of the Gunpowder Plot so I knew we had to put on a good show. The run up to bonfire was not smooth sailing all the way. We encountered the usual problems; ensuring the mammoth amount of money needed to put on the event was raised and getting enough volunteers each week for torch and faggot making. However, as expected the society came together and succeeded in putting on a spectacular event.

The author of this book, while known by many in the Battle area, was as such an outsider to Battle Bonfire Society. I hope that during his research he was made to feel welcome and that we didn't hinder him too much in his quest to find the best photos and stories from past and present members.

What Mick has managed to compile is a well-researched documentation of bonfire in Battle. Some parts you may have known before, some you probably didn't. Whether you are a hardened Bonfire Boy, a local who has attended for many years or someone with no knowledge of our society and its traditions I am sure you will find the book enjoyable.

What's more is that in buying this book (if you are reading this in the shop then go and pay for it) you are helping us maintain this traditional event.
Thank You.

Enjoy the book

Matt Southam
Hon Chairman

PRESENT DAY CHANT OF BATTEL BONFIRE BOYES

Remember, Remember the fifth of November,
The gunpowder treason and plot.
I see no reason
Why gunpowder and treason
should ever be forgot.
Guy Fawkes, Guy, t'was his intent
To blow up king and parliament.
Three score barrels were laid below
To prove old England's overthrow.
By god's mercy he was catch'd
With a darkened lantern and burning match.
Holla boys, holla boys, make the bells ring!
Holla boys, holla boys, God save the king!

Sussex Express 1906

Susssex Express 1906
"....next Tuesday is the immortal "Fifth" when, for some strange reason, all patriotic Britishers keep alive a memory of a happening over three hundred years old, which has been half as important or so far reaching in its effect as many another to forgotten event in our history........"

The AGM of 1905 was a typical of that era. On the night of the meeting The Battle Bonfire Boyes Drum and Fife Band marched down the High Street to the Star Hotel (the 1066 in today's money) entered the hostelry drums a bangin' and fifes a blowing. No doubt accompanied by a notorious 'Battle Rouser' or two. The upbeat and positive meeting announced there was a balance of £1.3s.5d. after an expenditure of £ 18 1s 7d.That is approximately £1000 in today's finance which to put into perspective is what the BBB spend on the fireworks for the effigy today. After the meeting there was a smoking concert and the health of the committee was healthy and heartily drunk. And then the following members Messrs Cruise, C. Stapley, W. Honeysett, G. Williams, R. Saxby, H. Parks, A. Thomas, J. Turner, F. Dowling, J. Holmes and W. O'Conner sang during the evening.'

DO TODAY'S MEETINGS HAVE THE SAME PASSION?
LETS ALL HOPE SO!

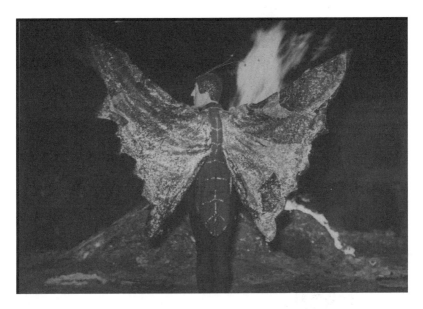

The Early Years

BANEFIRE–BONEFIRE–BONFIRE

According to the Oxford English Dictionary the word Bonfire came into use around 1755, peculiarly over 100 years after the major event its name is used to celebrate. Before this it was Bonefire or Banefire which seem to originate from Scotland.

"...annual midsummer banefire in the burgh of Hawick where old bones were regularly collected and stoved..."

This quote from 1463 seems to be the first recorded use of the word. This was a part of the dreamily romantic notion that burning bones would ward off dragons. Ever seen a dragon around a bonfire?

Although the original definition of the word may relate to a "fire of bones", there are two more meanings that are clearly more relevant.

A fire of immolation, a fire in which heretics, bibles or proscribed books were burnt.

A large fire kindled in the open air for a celebration.

Bonfire celebrations of some kind existed long before the notorious Gunpowder Plot. They were used by villages or parishes as a get together after a hard week's work and to celebrate various festivities. They were an excuse to enjoy oneself and a release from the everyday trudge of labour. Noise was a crucial element of these celebrations and it is likely that most people did not know exactly what they were celebrating. Saturday night, bonfire, good time was surely the philosophy of most celebrators. This is typified by Thomas Holland, professor at Oxford 1589–1612, concerning Bonfire celebrations,

"[To] be used by the people of this land only as a significant argument to express their sincere affection in joy"

If bonfires were not new, neither were November bonfire celebrations. The ancient Celtic festival "Samhain" meaning *Summer's End* was the first day of winter, and the end of one pastoral year. It was the time when the night became longer than the day, and the year began again with its dark winter half. Originally a Druidic festival, it was celebrated on the eve of November 1st. surprisingly there were also some association to Christian celebrations with churches sponsoring most of the events. As well as some dates in the Christian Calendar that had been hijacked or borrowed from the Roman and Celtic Calendars (For example, All Saints Day was simply the Roman Pantheon festival moved on in the medieval guise). There were also some new "Christian" celebrations in November. Included in this during in the 1570s was Queen Elizabeth I's birthday or "The Queens Holy Day". Celebrated on 17th November, throughout the land bells were rung, bonfires and illuminations were lit and much drinking was seen.

Although there is no suggestion that these events specifically evolved into the current festivities on the "Fifth", it is clear that they will have had some influence on the now traditional Guy Fawkes celebrations.

An integral part, interwoven with the early history of Battle Bonfire, is the manufacture of gunpowder in the local area. There are reports suggesting an industry in the area as early as the 1560s but the first reports we can specifically put against a gunpowder mill in Battle is 1676 when John Hammond obtained a grant to produce gunpowder in the area. At its height there were five mills in the surrounding area all built along the banks of the now small stream The Asten which winds its way around Battle. There was even a blend known as Battle Powder that was, *"a particularly good sporting powder"* And according to the **Victoria History of Sussex**, which quotes,

"The reputation of Battle factory was very high. Defoe mentioned that the town was remarkable for making 'the finest gunpowder and the best perhaps in Europe"

The industry ran successfully for almost two centuries finally closing in 1874 due to numerous fatal accidents. Without doubt the ease at which gunpowder was available helped the explosiveness of Battle Bonfire. This legacy of the gunpowder industry lives on with road names such as Powdermill Lane.

So with a reputation of being home to one of best gunpowders available and with the medieval fascination with bonfires and firework celebrations, there is every probability that bonfire, or Banefire, celebrations in Battle actually started well before The Gunpowder Plot.

Then 1605 comes along and the Gunpowder plot explodes on the scene, or nearly did. There are masses of words and heaps of books written about The Gunpowder Plot. To go into the intrigue and conspiracies or counter conspiracies of the event would turn this into an epic of mind numbing proportions. So to put it very briefly; On November 5 1605 a man was arrested in the cellars of Parliament House. Although he first gave his name as John Johnson, a series of events gradually unfolded under torture. Guy or Guido Fawkes, born April 13 1570 in York, was one of thirteen who had conspired to blow up Parliament, the King and his Lords, thereby throwing the country into turmoil. From this these men hoped to raise a new, sympathetic, monarch, and return England to its Catholic past. The conflicting historical details so far can only confirm one theory - that the official account of this event is probably not true. The debate over what the evidence means has been hotly contested by many people cleverer than me through the centuries, and continues to be an engaging enigma for today's historians.

Remember, Remember the fifth of November,
The gunpowder treason and plot.
.....the winner writes the history

To put this into some kind of perspective, this was not a one man's assassination attempt on the King. This was a minority terrorist group, allegedly sponsored by outside religious fanatics, attempting to destroy the home of King, Government and everything that represented civilisation of its day. It would have been the "9/11" of its era. Celebration of the failure of the plot started in London the following year by the ringing of bells and "much merriment." This soon spread out of the City and within four or five years was celebrated across the country but most evidence suggests that bonfire celebrations were not added until the 1630s.

BATTLE'S BEGINNINGS

The first recorded history of a Bonfire celebration in Battle is reputed to be as early as 1646, but the first authenticated mention of a Battle bonfire celebration in Battle is of 1686, when church warden's accounts showed 17 shillings and sixpence to be 'expended on gunpowder treason for rejoycings'. The church wardens were named Thomas Longley and John Hammond. (That is the same name as the man who had the first Gunpowder License in Battle.) Because then it was still a celebration against the failure of a Catholic plot the expenses of the 'fifth' was carried by the local parish.

What went on in the early life of Battle Bonfire up to the middle of the 19th century really has been lost in the ashes of many a bonfire. Very few, if any, records exist of this era. Any history really is only conjecture and assumption. As aforementioned, there is enough evidence to suggest that Battle held bonfire celebrations, unfortunately there seems no record of events over this period. Records imply that during the 18th century the celebrations lapsed, and that only a hardcore of places kept the celebration alive. There was a winter festival in Battle during the 17th and 18th century at the beginning of November so it is quite possible the Bonfire celebration was an integral part of that. Newspapers of the early 1800s do not seem to be too interested in local events. Local papers were more interested in national and international events or the price of pigs.

They were probably only read by the upper gentry (the only ones who *could* read) who had little interest in the working class celebrations. The beginning of this article in the local paper of 1865 might explain their views

> *"The predictions so often made that the custom of commemorating this day in this town would die out have not yet proved true; indeed we hesitate to believe that such will be the case, for we see each year that the movement is still supported by the inhabitants of the town and neighbourhood, and the celebrations are carried out without causing any breach of the peace or even calling for official interference. A contemporary may call it a "senseless exhibition" and refuse to give it publicity in the columns of his "penny paper," but there are other papers besides his which will give report of what he calls a "libel on the intelligence of the age."*

Reports of the Battle bonfire celebrations seem to start in the mid 1800s. This short report from the Sussex Advertiser from 1849 seems to be the earliest.

The Sussex Advertiser 1849

The gunpowder plot anniversary was celebrated here with Great Spirit. At nightfall a band of musicians perambulated the town, followed by a large company of torchbearers, some in costume of the traitor's (Guy Fawkes) time, and others in the most fantastic habiliments imaginable the effigy occupying an ospiscuis position in the midst. More than one of the bystanders coveted the skill of an artist to sketch the moving concourse, such a striking subject did it offer for the pencil, especially when passing into the Abbey grounds through the noble gateway, which was brilliantly illuminated by the bonfire on the Market Green. A continual discharge of rockets (That as far as pyrotechnics is concerned, reflected credit on the makers) added to the overall amusement. Much care was taken by the rocketers to avoid accidents. On the approach of a horse, for instance, "along the line of the signal ran," and the sport was instantly suspended. The whole was very well conducted.

The following year's report mentions "...how famed Battle is for the occasion ..." so it already had a history and reputation concerning Bonfire celebrations. Within ten years there were special trains arriving from Hastings

This could be the earliest photo of Battle bonfire.
Judging by the clothes, the fact the Green is grass and the bonfire is topped by tar barrels suggest this is around 1880s

transporting in excess of three hundred people.

Due to the lack of any records it is very difficult to pinpoint an exact time of formation of the Battel Bonfire Boyes (the spelling seems to change from year to year but this is the one used now) or Battle Bonfire Society. Bonfire Societies appeared in Sussex around 1815–30. There is no evidence to suggest anything different for BBB and it should be assumed that the birth of any resemblance to the modern society was around that time. The first actual mention of a committee is in 1860 but as this is not mentioned as anything new but by this time Battle already had a reputation for producing a good occasion. We should believe that there was an organising committee well before this time. At what point did the Church of England sponsored anti-catholic celebrations become the responsibility of an independent organisation committee? Nobody really knows.

1800s AND CATHOLICISM

During the mid 1800s the anti-Catholic feeling was still the driving force of the celebration. There is no reason to believe that this older and fuller version of the famous "Remember Remember …" was not being used.

Remember, Remember the fifth of November,
The gunpowder treason and plot.
I see no reason
Why gunpowder and treason
should ever be forgot.
Guy Fawkes, Guy, t'was his intent
To blow up king and parliament.
Three score barrels were laid below
To prove old England's overthrow.
By god's mercy he was catch'd
With a darkened lantern and burning match.
Holla boys, holla boys, make the bells ring!
Holla boys, holla boys, God save the king!
A farthing loaf to feed old Pope
A pennorth o' cheese to choke him,
A pint o' beer to wash it down,
And a faggot o' wood to burn him!
Burn him in a tub o' tar
Burn him like a blazing star,
Burn his body from his head

And then we'll say old pope is dead!
Hip, hip, hooray!

There is no hiding the sentiments in the last nine lines and also in this opening paragraph from the *Sussex Express* of November 1839 making a comment what 'the fifth' was all about.

> '....the day where on our fathers were used to yield their unfeigned thanks and praise for the wonderful and mighty deliverance of our King, Lords and Commons appointed by Popish treachery to the slaughter and the deliverance of our Church and nation from popish tyranny and arbitrary power....'

Twenty years later and little had changed. During the 1850 & 1851 celebrations there are reports of a man walking around in the centre of the procession with a talking trumpet, what ever that was, *repeating reminded the assembled throng of the origins of these manifestations of loyalty and aversion to gunpowder.* The *Sussex Express* of 1852 showed those feelings, especially in Sussex, were still riding high.

> 'Guy Fawkes treason is still commemorated here, and is likely to be while Papists continue their efforts to rule this Protestant country and threaten in the language of Joannes Bonus "Missionary Priest of the Archdiocese of Westminster," to "tar and feather" Protestant clergymen.'

This impassioned article was published in the local press in 1859 which itself was republished from the National Standard to prove then anti Catholic fever was still burning over 150 years after the Gunpowder Plot.

THE FIFTH OF NOVEMBER
(from the National Standard)

"Remember the fifth of November
Gunpowder Treason and Plot;
We see no reason why Gunpowder Treason
Ever should be forgot"

Parliaments may do their best to blot out the memories associated with the Fifth of November, but they cannot succeed. While England remains a free nation she must remember events and deliverance so closely connected with the vindication of her independence. We do not – we cannot – we dare not- forget the Fifth of November. Weak statesmen, whose faith rest on a transient party union, rather than on a protecting Providence may council oblivion of God's mercies; but we, who hold that He rules in the kingdom of the earth may not follow such unworthy counsels. Passing years do but increase our sense of the great blessing which He wrought for us when but for His overruling hand all that makes England great and free had gone to wreck...

...Forget the past! Forget His mercies! – We cannot, we dare not. For our only hope for escape from evils we foresee and which we deserve, is, that in days of bygone danger, God fought for England, and that "his mercy endureth for ever............"

By 1868 moderation had begun to transcend the anti-catholic feelings. Although a religious undertone existed, the celebrations moved more towards a merrymaking feeling. This opening address taken from that years' bonfire starts with traditional anti-catholic sentiments but closes with talk of *"rockets and merry a peal"*.

In olden time a traitor knave named Guy,
Conjointly with a Popish gang designed
That England's King and nobleman should die,
That Romish chains might English freedom bind.

But happily their schemes were all blown up,
The King's sagacity preserved the State;
The papists drank of disappointment's cup,
And Guy and partners shared the traitors' fate.

Now yearly as November's fifth comes round,
Good subjects will their loyalty reveal.
Old Battel in the van is always found,
With bonfire, rockets and a merry peal.

Some towns, devoid of spirit, make no moves,
We, to be foremost in the cause aspire;
Kind patrons aid our cause and time will prove
That Battel still retains its former fire.

Taken from "A Sussex Life.
The memories of Gilbert Sargent. Countryman"
By Dave Arthur

Although this address was taken from an era when much was changing in the celebrations, it is clear from the final verse that Battle was one of the few towns to keep its traditions and *"retains its former fire"*. The question to be asked is why was Sussex so anti catholic? And why did Battle keep those traditions alive? There is no definitive answer but maybe a few sparks can be thrown into the proverbial bonfire of ideas as to why the desire has been there.

At the time of the Gunpowder Plot, Sussex, though less than fifty miles from London, was, due to the North Downs and High Weald, an isolated county with a terrible infrastructure. It was known throughout the land for its terrible roads which were impassable in the winter months. Not only were the towns and villages isolated so were their ideas.

In the 17th century, Sussex had the highest population of Catholics in the land and according to Anthony Fletcher in his book *Sussex 1600–1660*, Battle was a "Hotbed of Popery" which included a centre for Catholic teaching. As can be seen by situations in today's world different cultures with different ideals can struggle to live in harmony.

As a coastal county there was always fear of an invasion from Europe. A Catholic Europe.

The manufacture of Gunpowder was widespread across Sussex.

The Abbey, while owned privately, was owned by friends of royalty so would support the celebrations.

These are not the reasons why Sussex, and especially Battle, held on to this event but this may help to understand why it has survived.

Within twenty years all this hostile reaction had dissipated and by the 1880 Battle bonfire had lost all its anti-Catholic feeling and moved on to a more modern base of just having a good time. The following report from the Daily News, a national paper from 1888, has no mention of any anti-Catholic feeling at all, in actuality it mentions that *"the original object was completely lost sight of...."* *(see p. 16)*.

As you can see with the use of hot air balloons, effigies and re-enactments of famous Battles the carnival philosophy had taken over. Oddly the only mention of a Sussex bonfire was at Eastbourne. Was this because the Anti

Daily News
6 November 1888

THE FIFTH OF NOVEMBER

Some attempt to keep up Guy Fawkes' Day was made in London; but the original object was completely lost sight of. Such effigies as were carried about were those of persons who have recently made themselves popular or notorious. Amongst a few political "guys" there was a large sprinkling of stuffed figures labelled "Jack the Ripper" or "Leather Apron." Sir Charles Warren also came in for some attention. At Hampstead the usual bonfire was lighted on the heath, in the presence of a crowd of visitors. There was also a procession of masqueraders. The annual carnival of the "bonfire boys" was held at Lewisham amid a good display of coloured lights, but the bonfire was dispensed with. At Eltham Mr. Parnell and other Irish members of Parliament were "guyed." In connection with a masquerade at Yeovil a balloon ascent was made, and a dummy was allowed to float down to the ground by means of a parachute in imitation of Baldwin. The descent is described as successful, and graceful. At Eastbourne several bonfires were lit and effigies of unpopular persons were burnt amidst a display of fireworks. At Salisbury a bonfire was lighted by the Mayor, and there was a display of fireworks. A torchlight procession in costume was organized at Bridgwater, and there was a mimic combat between H.M.S. Orlando and the Royal Horse Artillery with Roman candles. At Exeter the celebration was on a more extensive scale than has been the case of late years. "Young Exeter" and the guys marched in procession with lighted torches and accompanied by a band. In the roadway facing the west front of the Cathedral a huge bonfire had been erected, and on the arrival of the procession in the cathedral yard a light was applied to the pile and it was soon ablaze. There was also a display of fireworks.............

catholic feelings were still running high at the major two? Lewes, no doubt! And as for Battle's celebration for that year? Being the 300th celebration of the defeat of the Spanish armada it was highlighted by a tableau of Admiral Drake's ship and the effigy thrown on the fire was of some chap named Jackson, who murdered a prison warden. Not too controversial. To show how the party atmosphere had taken over within ten years there would be a German brass band playing in the procession. Considering this was an era when the local newspaper wrote a lengthy feature concerning an electric light outside Ticehurst & co, a butcher in the town, which everyone should go and see in the evening, the spectacle of the Bonfire and fireworks must have been mind blowing.

Fancy dress in the early 1950s

The Modern Era

1900 AND FORWARD

By the turn of the 20th century Battle bonfire celebrations had lost all sense of the anti catholic feeling and turned into a carnival but that does not mean it had lost any of its anti establishment feeling. And in fact the 1900s would create more problems than at any time in its history and on several occasions the very future of the event was in doubt.

The 20th century got off to a fine start as the *Sussex Express* report was all about jollity and the firework display was "a capital pyrotechnic display" and the Tableau was of a soldier in hospital in Veldt, South Africa. The other half of the tableau was his parents waiting at home. Topical and politically strong for its time. Over the next few years the "Fifth" seemed to be riding high on its own success. The committee meeting of 1905 agreed for the first time that it would give out prizes for the best fancy dress, even if they did give them all to committee members, it was an innovative idea that still exist today. As we shall see later, *BB and the Law*, this era would soon become Battle Bonfires toughest and there was a period which was probably the longest in history where there was no bonfire on its traditional home at the Green.

The celebrations restarted after the Great War in 1919. Even though they were fairly well supported there seems to doubt whether this is the right thing to do after such a momentous event. What was the relevance of celebrating an event 300 years ago after what happened in the last four years?

But carry on it did. Just this memory from an article in the *Sussex Express* of 1919 gives a little insight into the anticipation for the Battle Bonfire celebrations at the beginning of the 20th century. Spookily the author is a M. H. Hoad

> *...The "Fifth" to a Battle schoolboy prior to the war {WW1} was a red letter day. To the youth and young man it was an event long looked forward to with weeks of preparation for the carnival – and the preparation included "tell it not in Gath," the storing up of quantities of home made squibs – otherwise known as the notorious Battle Rouser. The old people looked forward also, and backward. The "Fifth" brought memories of bygone happier days...*

The 1920s proved to be a perplexing period for the BBB. All the A.G.M.s seem to cover the same problem. Lack of support. In 1924 and 1925 there was real doubt if there would be a celebration. In fact in 1924, only about 25% of the committee bothered to turn up for the bonfire celebrations. In 1929 the first meeting was not until 24th October! Bizarrely this is rated as one the best bonfire celebrations of that era. Maybe the modern society should try and organise an event in two weeks. Even stranger there were 138 entries into the fancy dress competition. Life seemed to being brought back into the event during the 1930s.The pubs applied for extended hours on bonfire night, they asked for the outrageous request for 6.00 opening, until 11.00 which was reluctantly agreed. By the mid 1930s reports of jostling crowds and tremendous turn outs dominated the papers. The 1933 celebrations had reports of 8,000 rousers being launched. And at the following year's celebrations, the "Rousers" were so powerful they flew over the top of the buildings leaving trails like comets. There is a report in the *Sussex Express* of a BBB meeting with a staggering 300 people in attendance. In 1935 a large airline "buzzed" the bonfire celebrations which were gratefully welcomed by the launch of bundles of rockets which bombarded the plane and lit up the sky. It is strange that life was about to take this concept to horrific reality. Of course all this optimism was to stop instantly. What was going on in world events put the Bonfire celebrations into it true perspective, and by 1939 the fifth was without fires: '...*young and old alike will regret the suspension of the carnival which is observed in this county on an unequalled scale...*' as the local news reported.

The bonfire celebrations survived the two world wars,

Programme from 1945

the second leading to probably its greatest period. As the world moved into a new era after WW2 the prevailing feelings had changed from WW1 when the attitude then seems more of a "no, we really shouldn't enjoy ourselves after such a momentous event" where in 1945 it had changed to "we really should enjoy ourselves after such a momentous event." As it was the end of the blackout and the first bonfire for seven years it was going to be a night not to forget. Everyone was encouraged to dress up to the point the BBB handed out five hundred fancy dress outfits to the public. Committee members were fined if not in attire. Add to this a massive one hundred pounds spent on fireworks which were launched for the first time from the top of the battlement. What a spectacular sight that must have made for the first time viewer. Additions over the next couple of years included massive floodlights erected to bathe the Green in light for the marching displays of which these were dominated by the iconic Dagenham Girl Pipers. Of course, Rousers made a return mixed in with the odd explosive left over from a recent event. Over the next six years the celebration would raise up to a climax of light and sound to which one reporter called "...a festival of light..." When asked about these celebrations those who witnessed them would always mention the noise. Thousands of Rousers were set off, added to the sounds of five or six marching bands always which was headed by BBB's own drum and fife band thundering their instruments in the confined space of the building lined High Street that holds in their memory.

Previously in 1933 the then chairman, Mr C.J.S. Norris, approached the BBC with the notion of recording the celebration of the Fifth events for broadcast. Their diplomatic reply was: "...difficult to reproduce 'on air' the atmosphere of the proceedings." By 1949 their view had

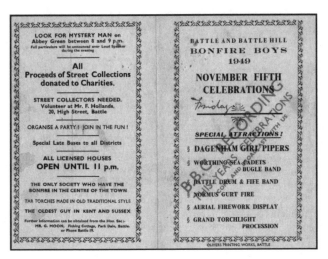

Programme from 1949. The event was
recorded by the BBC

changed and as the fire started to burn, BBC commentators
made descriptive recordings of the scene for broadcast to
Italy, Spain, France and even China. Also gaining his
impressions on that night was the Marquis de Visdelou-
Guimbeau (no idea who that is!) who was living at St.
Mary's Battle at the time. He broadcast a talk on the evening
pageantry to Canada, sending greetings to French-Canadian
ex-service men who were stationed near Battle during the
war. Unfortunately none of these recordings survive.
Fireworks on the radio, an interesting concept. To prove the
popularity of the event at this time British Movietone News
covered the bonfire between 1945–50 for national broadcast
in all cinemas.

By the beginning of the 1950s celebrities from Radio and
the new fangled television were often guest of honours. The
highlight being 1951 when the guest list included an
ambassador from Chile, Senor Don Manuel Bianchi, and
the Belgian ambassador, Vicomte Obert de Thieusies, the

A fancy dress competition

Marchioness Curzon of Kedleston, and Mr Marcus Cheke, vice marshal of the Diplomatic corps. Another guest that night was Mr Derek Bond, the film actor (he was in *Scott of the Antarctic* and 48 other films!). Asked for his view, the Belgian ambassador said "My Chilean colleague and I will always remember the evening we spent here. When we go back to our respective countries we will tell them all about it." Which really is the kind of quote which should have been lost in the mists of time, but is my duty to keep alive. No one asked the Catholic Chilean ambassador what his thoughts were on the proceedings.

It was in during this period in the late 1940s when Saturday became the celebration day almost by default, up to this date the celebrations were always held on the "fifth". In 1949 the 5th was on a Saturday, therefore in 1950 the 5th was on a Sunday and of course it had to be Saturday because Sunday was church day, and it seemed just stuck from there. Of course more volunteers could be called on to help on

Saturday as they were not working and more were needed on the Sunday for clearing up. There were a few cries of selling out by the traditionalist when the decision was made to keep the celebrations on a Saturday. But of course Saturday was always going to be the success. The only time the date has been significantly changed was in 1966 when the celebrations were held on 29th October to coincide with the 900th celebrations of the Battle of Hastings.

Up until the late 1960s the celebrations did not conclude on the Saturday. On the Sunday evening after the bonfire there was a service in St. Mary's Church when the church path had a welcome of torches and the BBB banner draped across it. The inside was illuminated by lighted torches and the readings were given by The President and Chairman of the BBB. How the church got round this non Christian

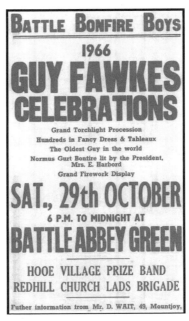

1966: The only time the date of the event has been siginifcantly changed

imagery is anyone's guess, or how many of the BBB made it on a Sunday after the night's revelry is not reported.

The 1970s and 1980s proved to have their own problems caused by the runaway success of the event (see *BB and the Law*), but the ever passionate BBB surmounted these to establish the format that runs to this day.

In the 21st century the event has to live with 21st century laws. Health and safety regulations have taken some of the edge away but not the enthusiasm of the BBB who have to face up to problems unimaginable to bonfire boys of the past.

ROUSERS

One of the most famous, or dare we say infamous, items in the history of Battle Bonfire was the Battle Rousers. This was a firework which was the creation of a local man named William Longley. That is the same family name as mentioned earlier in the first recorded mention of Battle bonfire. Are they the same family? Can this family claim a 400 hundred year association with the bonfire? William Longley worked for Brooks & Co, the famous fireworks manufacturer, and when he moved back into the town, he opened a barber's shop which was situated opposite the King's Head Pub. He applied for and got permission from the Chief Constable of Sussex Police to open his own fireworks manufactures, "William Longley Pyrotechnics", which opened for business in the mid 1880s. The wooden sheds, which were held together by copper nails to avoid sparks, were situated along North Trade Road where the modern school now stands. During this period Longley Pyrotechnics supplied and presented the fireworks display for the November 5th celebrations, his first being 1888. At the beginning of the 1890s William Longley Pyrotechnics offered their new firework invented specifically for the Battle celebrations, the Rouser. Innocent looking enough this was not just a firework with a bang. It had the unique feature that it would fly along the ground up to one hundred yards leaving a trail of white sparks before exploding in a cacophony of blinding light and deafening noise. The Rouser rapidly became

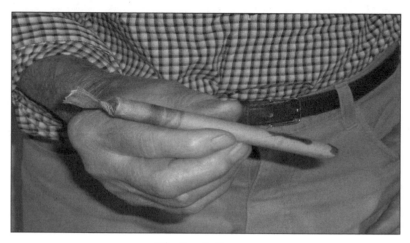

The Battle Rouser

a popular attraction at Battle Bonfire celebrations and as the work force at Longley Pyrotechnics were local and with the town's ironmongers Tills selling gunpowder over the counter, as it could in this era, it did not take long for Rousers to be made illegally at their homes by the workforce. By the turn of the century the Rouser had become one of the main attractions of the event with hundreds being launched each November 5th.

Hastings Observer Nov 14th 1891

William Longley, of 53 High Street was summoned for keeping explosives on his premises. When asked by Superintendent Smith if the defendant sold fireworks he answered yes. When asked to see the stock the defendant showed him a large number of fireworks in an iron box. He was told it was an illegal act to keep fireworks there with out registering the premises. Mr Longley said he thought the licence for his factory, which was a mile away, was sufficient. He was fined 1 shilling.

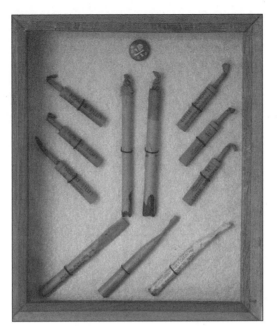

The rouser compared to commercially available bangers

The Battle Rouser was never anything officially to do with BBB. They were made independently from the society. It was never mentioned at BBB committee meetings, well not minuted anyway. It was something the committee would stand back from, although all the suspected makers were BBB members. When BBB went to other bonfire celebrations, people used to look forward to seeing and hearing the unique Rouser. But unlike the public, not all other societies welcomed the Rousers, especially Rye. Maybe this story, remembered by an established BBB did not help:

"...We visited a pub in Rye where the landlord was the brother of the Landlord of the Kings Head in Battle. We went and someone put down some Battle Rousers

and the pub had to close for the evening. The same thing happened at another pub we went to drink in."

Not the best thing for inter town relations. In fact BBB was not too keen on Rye celebrations because the Rouser would not run up the cobbled streets! Another story remembered by Fred Longley, of which he was present but would not admit to been a part of, but did have a big smile on his face when he told it:

"While having a drink one bonfire night in the Star hotel in its snug bar, which is a small welcoming bar that couples and more mature drinkers used to use. Noticing there was a large marrow on one of the window sills, the BBB who were present dually pierced it with a dozen rousers, 15 seconds later, accompanied by what could only have been a horrendous blast the snug bar had marrow on the ceiling, marrow on the floor, marrow on the customers, marrow everywhere!"

Of course the unpredictability of the Rouser was its great asset as well as causing its eventual downfall. They were generally tied up in dozens and when lit they would fly off in all directions. One of the most popular spectacles was putting two or three gross in a large circle, one brave BBB would go in light the lot and retreat to a safe haven and watch the dozens explode in a cacophony of noise and light. How loud? It was noted that the next village, Catsfield, a mere five miles away could hear the explosions on bonfire night. Unfortunately a Rouser could just as easily fly off into the crowd and injure. Various stories of lucky escapes survive. Tales of Rousers climbing up trouser legs and exploding were not unusual. Another slightly unusual story is of a BBB having a Rouser in his top pocket not noticing a spark igniting it and going off and blowing the bottom of his ear off! But the bottom line was it was a dangerous and illegal pursuit. One renowned incident happened not on bonfire night but was relevant in the fact that it showed the dangers of firework making. It was for the Coronation of George VII. Two men, who will remain nameless, were working out doors making the cases. They moved inside, switched on a light which created a spark and caused the powder drying to explode; killing the first man in and critically injuring the other who was in hospital for three months. It blew out all the windows in the house, blew off the front door and made the house unstable. Even this incident did not stop the dedicated few from making them, but after that incident Rousers were always made in daylight. Firework making is a dangerous pastime as this report from the *Sussex Express* of Nov 6th 1852 shows:

> *A deplorable accident happened last Wednesday, at the dwelling house of Mr Sadler, formerly The Bell beer house. His children were making fireworks and empted some damp gunpowder into a hot pan to dry. The pan unluckily, over heated, and the powder on coming in contact with it exploded. A large number of rockets ignited, and by the violence of the explosion the house became partly unroofed, and the three children injured, one of them so much her life is endangered.*

The Rouser was finally laid to rest in 1951. During the so called "Golden Era" of the late 1940s the reputation of the Battle bonfire was so high that a member of the committee was invited onto the BBC to talk about the bonfire celebrations. Innocently he took with him a few Rousers to enhance the review. Of course the sight was spectacular with Rousers rattling around the confines of the BBC car park. This demonstration was witnessed by the major firework manufactures who complained to the Home Office that this concept of a firework flying along the ground before exploding was illegal for them to produce. So they pressured the right people to get them banned once and for all and within the year the Firework Act of 1951 was introduced. There is no mention of any specific fireworks in the Act but it covers all grounds by saying that a firework manufacturer has to have a licence and must work in controlled conditions. The steps taken towards this end saw "Tills", the local ironmongers, prohibited from selling gunpowder. The BBB were sent a letter stating that the Rouser was now illegal (remember the Rouser was not officially anything to do with BBB) and the penalty for possessing them was imprisonment. Fred Longley, grandson of William Longley and the last surviving rouser maker, whose first bonfire he went to was in 1927 when he was five dressed, ironically, as a policeman, recalls:

> "I was heart broken when they said the Rouser was banned ...the police came round to my house to confiscate Rousers. They didn't know what they were looking for so I gave them a couple of dozen and off they went happy. Not worrying about the cases of them I had hidden under the manhole cover in the garden."

Another member, a relative of Don Waite remembers

> "When he lived in Mount Street a Policeman come up to ask hopefully they were not making fireworks, of course not was his reply, so the policeman decided to sit

outside and have a smoke. He sat on an ottoman which unbeknown to him contained over 400 rousers, and had his smoke, while those in the house held there breath hoping it wouldn't explode, which would have ignited the gunpowder which was baking in the Oven."

The Rouser builders discussed whether they should defy the ban, but as the penalty was imprisonment and the police were aware who were making them, and took a hard line, the decision was agreed by all that production should cease. The last few that escaped confiscation lived the following year, 1952, and then the Rouser flew no more. It is rumoured that one prominent Rouser maker buried all his Rouser making equipment deep in his garden, where it remains to this day.

At its death the formula for the Rouser was a closely guarded secret:

We had to have stiff paper for the cases, so we used old ledger sheets. These were rolled on stair rods which were cut to length. When the cases were made we rammed the powder into them. The police were listening for any sound of ramming. When the paper was rammed in, the touch paper had to be stuck on and the ends sealed with liquid pitch.

That is the closet you will get to the modus operandi of a Battle Rouser and as BBB pass on it is believed only one man Fred Longley, the grandson of the inventor is the last living owner of the knowledge. On many occasions he has refused to pass on this knowledge so one day this secret will only be known in the great firework display in the sky. Gone for all time.

From its initial ignition to its final explosion The Battle Rouser had a life from 1890 to 1952. Taking out two wars it only had a life of less than fifty bonfire celebrations. It had taken sixty years for the authorities to finally get its foe, a short reign for a lifetime of reputation.

1951 Fireworks Act

The Explosives Act is the oldest legislation enforced by the Trading Standards Service.

BATTLE BONFIRE AND
THE LAW

The bonfire celebrations have not always been at ease with the law and lawmakers. Today's site with the bonfire and fireworks set in a natural amphitheatre with the Abbey's ruins as a backdrop makes an impressive sight, but the traditional home for most of the history of the celebrations is on the Green in front of the historic Abbey Gates. But on more than one occasion the Bonfire has been moved from the venue. After a notorious Lewes Bonfire celebration of 1905 East Sussex County Council decided that it would up hold the Highway act of 1835 and the Explosive act of 1875 to the letter of the law and issued the following statement.

Statement from East Sussex County Council 1905
An important report from the Standing Joint Committee with reference to the bonfire celebration at Lewes on November 5th will come before the East Sussex County Council at their meeting on Tuesday. The committee state that they have had before them a report by the sub-committee appointed to consider the matter of the petition and counter-petitions with respect to the bonfire celebration at Lewes. The sub-committee stated that they had met and had heard the statements of the representatives of the petitioners and of the counter-petitioners, and while giving credit to the

various bonfire societies for a desire to minimise the evils pointed out by the petitioners, they were satisfied that the statements made by the latter were well founded, and they pointed out that the throwing, casting, or firing of any fireworks in or upon any highway, street, thoroughfare, or public place was subjected by the Explosives Act, 1875, Sec. 80, to a penalty of £5, and by the Highway Act, 1835, Sec. 72, the making or assisting in making any fire within 50 feet of the centre of any carriage way to the injury, interruption, or personal danger of any person travelling thereon was subjected to a penalty of 40s. Moreover, that the making of any bonfire in any street to the obstruction, annoyance, or danger of the residents or passengers was by the Towns Police Clauses Act, 1847, Sect. 28, subjected to a penalty of 40s., and constables were required to take into custody persons who within their view commit this offence. The sub-committee also called attention to the power given to the justices by the Licensing Act, 1872, Sect. 23, to make an order closing licensed houses where any tumult is apprehended.

The committee having carefully considered the report of their sub-committee, it was resolved that, as the lighting of bonfires and the letting off of fireworks in the streets is illegal, the same must be stopped throughout the county, and that the Chief Constable be instructed to take proceedings against all persons so offending, and further that it be ordered that due notice of his intention to do so should be posted and copies handed to the various representatives of the Bonfire Societies.

The basic facts were Sussex County Council banned all

Bonfire celebrations in the county within fifty feet of its roads, Battle celebrations were held on the Abbey Green, of course which was within that restriction. How would the Boyes react? Would they challenge or would they comply? At the following AGM of 1906, BBB had to decide what their action would be. There were many deliberations on whether the celebrations should go ahead. Chairman James Oliver responded with the following statement,

"County Council determined to suppress the celebrations of the "Fifth" especially with the regard to Fireworks in the street. It appears that they in Battle were to suffer for the sins of others.{Lewes} He could say without the fear of contradiction that the bonfire celebrations for the last four of five years at the least had been carried out in the most orderly of manner, and the Superintendent of police and his men had no cause of complaint whatsoever. ...of course they did not wish to disobey the law in any way, and it almost made them down hearted. He did not see why if they did celebrate the "Fifth", why they should not get fuel for the bonfire. He trusted if they had their celebration no member of the society would let off fireworks in the street."

The Members decided unanimously in favour of celebrating the fifth, "so much as the Law would allow." They agreed they would accept the ruling as they did not want to breach the law and all members agreed that no fireworks would be thrown in the street. The celebrations carried on with over a hundred members in the procession, with all the usual enthusiasm, including a firework display, still organised by William Longley Pyrotechnics. There were no problems, in fact reports state the High Street was "unwontedly quiet" after the procession had passed. The only concession was the bonfire was moved from its traditional place in front of the Abbey to Wellington field, north of the High Street. No doubt kept in order by the extra police drafted in by the local constabulary. All four of them! The only real conflict with controversy was the tableau which was a 'Battle Rouser' fitted with a muzzle and guarded by four soldiers. This may have been the first time since the gunpowder plot that there had not been a bonfire on the Green on the Fifth.

What happened the following year is a little vague. Knowing a bonfire on the Abbey Green was banned, some reports suggest that BBB disbanded others suggest that they choose to not celebrate the 'fifth'. What did happen is the Battle Hill Bonfire Boys arose and eventually took up the official mantle of keeping the Battle Bonfire active. The BHBB held their bonfire celebrations basically along the same lines as the BBB, visiting the same places, including the Abbey, delivering the chant and a procession around the town using a very similar route. With their bonfire situated off Old Lane, which was some where on Battle Hill, the bonfire was away from the public road so the restrictions from the County Council did not apply. Over the next few years BHBB kept the show alive, but always there were little afters. As the Battle Hill celebrations had concluded the events moved to the unauthorised efforts in the High Street to keep the tradition alive. This report from the *Sussex Express* from 1907 showed that members of the BBB did their utmost to keep the tradition alive on the Green

Sussex Express 1907
...In the High Street groups of men were dotted here and there, and youths patrolled the streets in groups and now and then an outburst of Rousers sounded through the streets, and those responsible for their

ignition kept themselves hid. It is true, one or two boys were caught red handed and had to disclose their identity and their place of residence to a vigilant officer of the law. A silent and unsuspicious looking crowd was assembled outside the George Hotel, and at times more exploding Rousers were lit by unseen hands. Then a shout went up. The walls of the grand old Abbey were illuminated by a dancing and bizarre light. A fire on the Green had been lit. The quiet crowd suddenly became a noisy mass and stampeded helter skelter to the Abbey Green. Here matters for a moment looked suddenly somewhat serious. A tar barrel, filled with inflammable material, was lit in one of the passages on the side of the Green, and was rolled on to the road. A policeman however was at hand and somewhat unwisely – doubtless hoping to nip the problem in the bud – attempted to roll the barrel back and in doing so its flaring contents came on to the pavement close to a fence and in a short time the fence was ignited. The houses at this point are small and partly timber built and looked as if there would shortly be a serious catastrophe, but a number of men shovelled the now flaring mass into the roadway and managed to extinguish the flaring fence, but while endeavouring to stop all danger to the property, they were determined to have their fire, and the flaming tar was scrapped into a heap, and was soon augmented by a faggot or two, and later by the tar barrel which the police, presumably not knowing quite what to do with it, relinquished, then by innumerable boxes, an old couch and several old chairs, hampers, straw and hedge clippings, in fact anything that would burn was brought by willing hands from all quarters, and the police, after their first brave attempt to maintain order, stood by and looked on, and even they had to smile at the efforts of the "Battlers" to have a good "fire on the green." The crowd though determined, was an exceedingly good humoured one, and beyond making a deal of noise singing and shouting around their impromptu fire, and a well- maintained defiance of the law in the matter of fireworks, did no damage. The celebration, considered by those who took part as a worthy of the best traditions of the town, concluded about midnight.

By 1911 the BBHB had become the establishment as the torch lit procession now included the famous old Guy, which made a move to the Battle Hill Bonfire Boys. The following year, probably for reasons of jealousy of the success of the Battle Hill Bonfire Society, the BBB re-emerged and in conjunction with the BHBB organised that year's celebrations. After numerous meetings between various groups agreement was reached to allow an official bonfire back on the Green for the first time since 1906. A highly respectable one hundred and thirty society members dressed up in fancy dress. Lady Webster, the then owner of Battle Abbey, lit the fire. The famous Battle "Rouser" made a return to the High Street and was much in evidence in spite of the vigilance of the police. Even though the celebrations were a success this was a false dawn for the return of the fire on the Green. Of all things a public footpath was to be its demise. The bonfire did have opponents and with the County Council insistence in its upholding the Highway act of 1835 and the Explosive act of 1875 to the letter of the law, the discovery of public footpaths across the green was the justification needed to deem the bonfire illegal. The BBB committee after consulting solicitors, who advised them that any official bonfire sponsored by the Bonfire Boyes would be illegal on the Green and the committee would be liable for prosecution, unsurprisingly decided not to hold a fire on the Green but would go ahead with the all the other festivities. Inexplicably, a load of wood and paper was dumped on the Green during the day by "somebody". A bonfire to be built? There was a notably long procession with a typically political tableau, a woman labelled "the height of impudence; I want the vote". The route around the town was lined by hundreds who had arrived from Hastings and other surrounding villages, which included plain clothed police. As the procession moved around the town small fires were lit along the route. The few who risked lighting fireworks in the streets were quickly arrested. After the

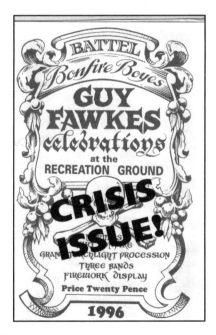

The Battel Bonfire has been close to being cancelled in the past

procession had cleared the High Street, the stack of wood and paper on the Green was lit and several men pushed a cart full of faggots down the high street, which was hastily added to the fire. After "some hustling," most of the men where arrested while others disappeared down the alleys in the back of the cart. As these men were led away by the police a barrel of tar appeared and was deposited on the fire. Battle again had defied the odds and law to have a bonfire. After all the conflicts and law changes which allowed only one authorised bonfire on the Green in the preceding eight years world events took over and all Fifth celebrations across the country ceased for the duration of the Great War.

In 1919, in a changed world, the debate started on the proposal of reviving the fifth celebrations. There had not been a celebration on the Green for seven years and only one in the previous twelve, so it was far from a foregone conclusion. There was a strong feeling within a section of the public in what was the relevance of an event three hundred years old compared to what had happened in the world over the last few years. Was it right to go out and party and enjoy themselves when thousands failed to survive? The BBB did decide to hold a celebration, the suggestion that the bonfire should be on Armistice Day, November 11th, was put forward and rejected. The County Council's attitude to bonfires had also drifted out of the equation and a bonfire was erected on the Green with no complications.

The next time the bonfire was forced off the green was for World War 2. Of course, the blackout and war meant that the bonfire could not go ahead even if there was anybody who wanted it to. Partly to keep the tradition alive, a show of defiance against the enemy and in memory of fallen Bonfire Boyes on the fifth a single candle was placed in the middle of the Green.

The final time the bonfire celebrations were held on the

Abbey Green was in 1995. Due to renovation work by English Heritage the Gatehouse was covered in scaffolding and it was deemed not safe to have a Bonfire on the Green. The opponents of the Bonfire, and there were and still are many, saw this as an opportunity to get the bonfire moved or even stopped. So for the 1996 event an alternative venue had to be found. After many meetings the Recreation Ground, was agreed. Probably not known by many Bonfire Boyes, but in fact the very same site where the last Battle Bonfire off the Green was held ninety years earlier. Even though the site was popular with the majority of BBB it turned out to only be a temporary measure. So again the following year, a new site was needed and eventually today's permanent home on Senlac Field, the site of the Battle of Hastings was agreed.

The relationship between BBB and English Heritage, the owners of Battle Abbey, at times has been strained but it is the best for both parties to make this work. BBB have to accept that a return of the full celebrations on the Abbey Green is a non starter and is it not English Heritage's mandate to save England's heritage

Bonfire celebrations and, especially Battle, has a reputation of rowdiness and violence. In all the research done for this book one statement has come up regularly concerning the bonfire celebrations at Battle. There has been little or no violence compared to activities at other celebrations. As we have already seen in the newspaper report of 1865 it states that "*.. no breach of peace or even calling for official interference...*" Old BBB, even if they are a little biased, do not remember any trouble, apart of a bit of drunkenness. Some members get agitated when the subject of violence is mentioned. Even the police remember very few real troubled moments but the bonfire celebrations still carry an undeserved reputation for violence. To say it has been an afternoon tea party would also be a fallacy.

What is constituted as violence? Are a few fireworks going off in places they should not be construed as violence?

One perception that has stuck with BBB and, in fact has, almost been encouraged, is the amount of fireworks let off in the street. With the history of the Rouser and the noise of other fireworks and maybe the reputation has grown out of this. This little tale remembered in 1919, by a Miss Harvey, a very old lady at the time and a granddaughter of a former proprietor of the Battle Gunpowder Works, tells of an era before the Mills closed in 1874, which gives a small insight to what the atmosphere must have been like in the mid to late 19th century on the "Fifth" in Battle.

> "*At Battle on Guy Fawkes Day every workman at the powder Works got a certain amount of gunpowder to celebrate the event, and residents of Battle never answered a knock on the door after dark, as a squib or some other firework would be hurled in.*" She also said, "*if any man had a grudge against anyone in Battle, they paid it off very unpleasantly that night*"

To add to the evidence that small grudges were evened on bonfire night this incident reported in the *Sussex Express* of Nov 7 1866 of a court hearing of three "young men" who were charged with "wilfully breaking a pane of glass in a window at Battle Grammar School" at the lodgings of the Principal Mr Wm. Lamborn. A Robert Gant was found guilty of lighting a squib and throwing it at the window.

The damage was	2s 6d
He was fined	4s 3d
Damages	2s 6d
Cost	13s 3d

He immediately paid, but was still taken into custody and had to do a series of public duties

The opening segment of this letter sent to The South East Advertiser from the same era, 1876, also gives a another insight of what the Bonfire was like almost one hundred and fifty years ago, even before the time of the Battle Rouser.

Battle Gas V the bright moon and the torchlight procession

"Will or will not the august and select committee of our infused and very local Board again promulgate their decree for the town lamps to be lit upon this approaching anniversary, as we done last year and the years previous?

Although every possible care is taken by the acting committee of the bonfire boyes and indeed all its members, to avoid damage to property, it becomes nearly impossible to prevent strangers, who flock to our little town from all parts, hurling squibs and other explosives at such fair mark as alighted lamp, surrounded by glass processions, to deliberately court such damage, and why our harmless and loyal observance of the old fifth be ignominiously stamped out.

I can remember the 5th of Nov for the last 30 years, and can safely say that, since the introduction of Gas until a year or two ago, the lamp glasses were invariably removed, the gas not lighted upon these evenings, wisely, in order not to put temptations in the way

To put in to simple words he means, are they taking the gas lamps off because they get smashed on Bonfire night. So there was a little boisterousness or even a little wilful damage but nothing on the scale of other events.

1953 a report from Mr F.W. Evans Battle Chamber of Commerce to Battle Parish Council;
...that the local chamber of commerce would be removing the seats they had given the town on November 4th and replacing them on November 6th as they didn't want to see the on the bonfire

There was a fear in 1964 that the town was going to be swamped by Mods and Rockers using Battle bonfire as the latest venue for their latest disagreement on fashion and motorbikes. All the preceding week, rumours and gossip buzzed the town the Bonfire celebrations were going to be ruined by the next installment of battles over different styles. Fortunately nothing materialised and the celebrations went ahead successfully.

Moving on 35 years, there was a period, especially in the late 1980s and 1990s when Battle success was nearly its downfall. For anyone who has not visited Battle, it is a one street town completely enclosed by buildings. There were times in this period when twenty thousand people were compressed into the small rural town. The thought of that many people squeezed into that space is frightening. The newspapers at the time certainly seemed to dwell on an anti-bonfire feel in the way they reported the event more than any other time in its history. More often than not the reports were solely centred on the violence of the event. Looking back at various reports of scuffles and even a stabbing and one insurgence of a group of fascist/skinheads types setting on a couple of black youths and counter reports of over zealous policing we would have thought the

Plaque marking the site of the bonfire, the site of the Battle of Hastings

William Longley, inventor of the Battle Rouser.

His grandson, Fred Longley, and last surviving rouser builder

The important job of erecting the centre post as it was done in the 1950s

The same job 50 years later in 2005

The faggots are quickly assembled into positon ready for the bonfire.

The oldest Guy in the world?

Excitement is in the air as the 2005 effigy is revealed; a selection of rockets with the faces of the conspirators on!

1977 saw a new development to the celebrations, the burning of an effigy.

The spectacular fireworks display

The youngsters get involved   *The fire juggler*

The bonfire is lit!

event had turned into anarchy. To put things into the right frame of mind, this was the era of Thatcherism and miners strikes. There was rioting on the streets of Liverpool and Birmingham and football hooliganism was rife. So when a town the size of Battle had over fifteen thousand squeezed into its one street it was not surprising that the police were a little anxious. The editor of the local press at the time blamed all this on BBB.

Of course, it was not all doom and gloom. Ask the people who were there and no one can tell you when these violent events occurred. During these times of heightened passions, the mid 1980s are held high in the memories as some of the best celebrations of the modern era. For example 1984, had a huge turn out of participants in the procession, five bands, Morris dancers, re-enactment societies plus a plethora of other bonfire societies topped off by exploding Margaret Thatcher and Arthur Scargill, the hero and villain of the time; make your own decision which was which. This caused BBB Legend Bert Goble, 76 at the time, to comment "this is my forty ninth Battle Bonfire and the best I've ever been to."

In fact by the mid to late 1990s the success of BB was becoming its own worst enemy. The numbers attending were getting out of hand as concerns from the Bonfire Boyes were voiced about organisations earning profit on the back of their charitable event. The Bonfire Boyes expressed anger at British Rail's policy of running trains every half an hour from Hastings and Tunbridge Wells. There where incidents when emergency vehicles could not get through the town solely because of the number of people. This really was a major disaster waiting to happen. Thankfully for everyone concerned it was a promise that was never fulfilled here.

This was also the time when there was a slight change of

Re-enactment socities were part of some of Battle's most memorable celebrations

policy concerning the policing of the event. There was thinking in police circles at the time that bonfires should be banned, and for the 1995 celebrations, a riot squad was stationed in Battle for the night armed with gas canisters, riot shields and helmets. They were very few incidents and the riot squad was not needed. The head of Battle police at the time an Inspector Harmer admitted he felt uncomfortable at the rather hostile look of the special unit. Later the question was asked at the town council if that was the way to police basically a family event. The riot squad was not used again.

As we have seen due to other circumstances the Bonfire was moved off the Green, there is little doubt the safety aspect was a major contributor to that decision.

To show how times and attitudes had changed, for the celebrations ninety years earlier, of 1905, when there was fears of trouble the head of Battle police, the wonderfully named Superintendent Plumb drafted in three extra policeman.

Retired local bobby, Mike Hedges remembers arriving in Battle in 1972 not ever hearing anything about Battle Bonfire or any other bonfire and was not sure what all the fuss was about on his first night. Over the next sixteen years he has a collection of memories of the event which broke the routine for a small town policeman. He has no memories of any real trouble and on most occasions enjoyed it. On the night of the bonfire he remembers having a NYPD Blues type briefing, which used to focus on the Public Order Act and the Firework Act. They would be a quick conversation with the Fire Brigade and the Ambulance Service. Unlike today's policing with modern technology policing was done on foot amongst the crowds. Two things use to worry him, the public used to bring young babies to the celebrations, and selling of fireworks to the underage.

What looked to others like a picking on the young and weak was in fact targeting the young so they would not get hurt. But he did admit that when fireworks were confiscated most of them would be let off in the backyard of the police station later in the evening. He remembers being selected to march in front of the procession on numerous occasions, which was a very responsible place as from there the pace of the procession was dictated. Once, while leading the procession past the Chequers pub "some blighter" lit a rocket nearly taking off his head. Was it aimed at the local Bobby by someone with a grudge? Let's hope not.

Another year, when he was in the front of the procession, by this time things had progressed so he was not on foot but in an old Morris Minor Van. He had been warned the battery was a bit iffy but with the true British spirit ignored that and carried on. His partner for the night was "a rather dishy WPC" who he tried to impress with his local knowledge and stressed the importance of their position at the front of the procession, as you do. Everything started well with the police van leading the procession down a noisy high street. Right in the middle of the procession route, right in front of the Green, right in front of the bonfire and thousands of people, right on cue the van's engine died, with the procession all stalled up behind. Whatever they tried the van would not restart and the more he tried the crowd burst into spontaneous cheers! Rejoicing and laughter was everywhere. Forever the gentleman, he asked the WPC if she get out and push the van. A few members of public and the first rank of bonfire boys tried to push start it. It refused. After much more baying from the crowd, eventually they decided to push into the local garage where it was abandoned and the procession could wind its merry way, by which time the WPC had disappeared and left him on his own. His mission to impress the young WPC was a complete failure. He reported back, sheepishly, to his Superintendent who implied he had let the side down and was a bloody idiot. Luckily the next day was his day off and by Monday it had all calmed down.

One of the major fears from our local bobby was always of drunks falling in the fire. After the public had wandered away and fuelled maybe by a little to much alcohol the ashes of the bonfire were very hot and one slight stumble could be fatal. In time past there used to be a BBB unspoken tradition of walking the ashes similar to the Polynesian island tradition and a very exclusive membership of BBB who had walked through the Ashes. There are tales of people who never quite made it and receiving horrific burns. This is one tradition that is not recommended to be revived. **Do not try this at home folks!!!**

NORMUS GURT AND GUYS

Battle bonfire celebrations have always advertised as having a 'Normus Gurt' bonfire. So what constitutes a "Normus Gurt" bonfire? Unlike some other societies, Battle's bonfire is built to a carefully prepared procedure built to an aged old plan to enhance the stability and burning and not just a big pile of rubbish. Stories of the bonfire being at least thirty feet high have been noted. In 1934 when the fire was alight the flames "leapt higher than the two towers of the gatehouse." And the following year a motor cycle standing in the roadway beside the Abbey Green caught fire and so fierce was the blaze that "...pleasure seekers encircling the bonfire were scorched by its heat." Even in the 1960s a letter of complaint was sent to the BBB from a home owner near the Green because the paint on his window frames began to blister. Also, on more than one occasion the Abbey Green had to be repaired because the heat of the fire melted the tarmac. Eventually an area of fire resistant cobbles was mounted on the Green to protect it.

On other occasions the contents of the fire has caused a few problems. Up to the early part of the 20th century the fire was topped off not with a Guy but a barrel or two of tar, and on more than one occasion, a few were added into the faggots to encourage burning. This must have caused an interesting aroma but in 1912 it nearly set the High Street alight when a barrel rolled off the bonfire into a garden of

Bonfire building around 1930

one of the houses around the Green and set the fence and building alight. Only the quick thinking of a few police stopped it turning into something more damaging.

In 1958 the bonfire was built by Jack Waite and Dave Hurly, unfortunately maybe they started their celebrations a little too early and within an hour of it being built the tilting bonfire collapsed and it had to be rebuilt very quickly. In 1963 someone came up with the bright idea of topping the bonfire off with a dozen car tyres. And on more than one occasion the faggots got so wet the High Street was blanketed in thick smoke. People who visited in 1991 are still getting the smell out of their clothes.

It was only in the fairly recent history, in the last thirty years or so that the bonfire has been cleaned up on Sunday morning. It used to smoulder and live for another four or five days after the celebrations often kept alive by adding of fuel overnight. It was on the morning after; in the ashes of the bonfire that the remnants of various things were discovered.

Mattress springs used to sprout up overnight like mushrooms and the burnt remains of unwanted furniture was often to be found. One rumour persists, and no one will deny or confirm, that once a car which needed to be disposed off was put on the Green and the bonfire was strategically built around it.

In the weeks up to "The fifth", hundreds of torches for

the procession and faggots for the bonfire are made at a
secret location just out of the town. The traditional method
still used today has hardly changed over the years as these
pictures show. There used to be a large mill in town where
the workers used to "borrow" sacks to make the torches.
When the mill closed the owner offered the BBB a mass of
sacks not knowing he had been supplying them for years.

Apparently long time torch maker and life long Bonfire Boy Don Waite (left in the pictures opposite) and still making torches nearly forty years later (centre in picture below) would not let anybody near the dipping tank as it was his job to tar the torches. By all accounts the aroma from the tar would waft after him for weeks after Bonfire night.

BBB major claim is that the old Guy, affectingly known as Pear Head to older Bonfire Boyes, because the Head is carved out of Pear wood is the "oldest guy in the world" and that it is over 200 years old. Is there any evidence to suggest that this is the fact?

Guys for topping the bonfire did not appear until well into the 18th century and apart from the fact they are called guys there is little proof that Guy Fawkes was the original patron of this concept. The fact they are called guys is a strong argument but there is no evidence that this was the original name or that it was not something that rose out of Victorian ideals. Again there are plenty of theories on the

Tarring the torches

origins of guys but looking at the history of Battle bonfire it seems that it was not until the early 20th century that an image of Guy Fawkes was regularly sent to the flames. Other subjects were targeted for effigies, during the Crimean War for example, effigies of the Emperor Nicholas were far more highly praised than the representation of members of the Gunpowder Plot and there is more than enough records noting politicians and other villains other then Guy Fawkes regularly being banished to a fiery death.

And the original question is the guy 200 years old? Well possibly. *"An effigy of "Poor Old Guy" followed; and the rear was brought up by lines of torch-bearers,"* was reported in the 1850 *Sussex Express*. Was it old Pearhead? The first what we could call authenticated report is in 1900 when "the old effigy of Guy Fawkes was carried around the town" And of course the picture taken in front of the Abbey Gates

The guy from 1895
(with Rouser inventor William Longley on right)

The oldest guy in the world?

in 1895 is pictorial proof.

It is reported that in 1905 that an upholsterer, a Mr Barrow, whose shop was on the Green, rebuilt the body because of the poor condition. It had a 'new uniform and a repaint' in 1963. It was also rebuilt in 1984 by Max Blackman. So Pearhead definitely has a history. In 1900 it was "old". In 1849 "...*some in costume of the traitor's (Guy Fawkes) time, and others in the most fantastic habiliments imaginable the effigy occupying an ospiscuis position in the midst.*" And any reports say "the oldest guy in the world at least 200 years old." It seems that in some time periods, and it is reported in 1860, the head was removed from the body and the body was consigned to the fire.

BBB were reluctant to let me take it apart to see if any name is embezzled on it. Surely if you went through the trouble of carving this head you would have left your mark on it somewhere. Is it 200 years old? We have evidence of it being old at the turn of the 20th century. So we know it is over 100 years old (well the head anyway). It would have been a good

Life long bonfire boy Don Sergeant lights the bonfire

statement to make a lasting memento on the 200th anniversary of 1805 what about a head that would last another 200 years. Is it the oldest guy in the world? Where are the other contenders?

Don Sergeant used to keep the Guy in his Rouser making shed. One windy night he was in his shed and the Guy started moving from side to side. "He we go" he thought, the spirit of Guy Fawkes had returned to reap revenge for all those years of being banished to the flames. Having raised the courage to attack the Guy he found that there were six mice nesting in its body.

A slight modification on the Guy theme was offered in 1956 when an escapologist 'The Great Omani', offered to be a human guy and be tied to the centre of the fire as it was lit. His act was to escape unharmed before the fire really took hold and appear triumphantly on the Green.

BBB rejected the offer.

TABLEAUX AND EFFIGIES

Tableaux seemed to have been a part of Battle Bonfire Celebrations for as long as there have been celebrations. The earliest record of an individual tableau was in 1866 which was a representation of Count Bismarck. This was not mentioned as anything new so logic would dictate that the history is older. Tableaux at Battle Bonfire over this period were as diverse as they were ingenious as subjects included one of Admiral Drake's ships, the Anglo/Japanese agreement of 1905 to the local grievance of the muzzled Battle Rouser and of course, good old Guy Fawkes reared his head at regular intervals. It seems in this period that BBB built their own tableau and even had it presented on a stage built on the Green. In 1889 the tableau was original in design and form. It featured Charles I being taken around the town on a handcart within the procession. At various points on the route a little act would be performed which ended with the Monarch being beheaded.

In the 20th century the idea of one major tableau sponsored by the BBB for the bonfire seemed to morph into a collection of mobile tableaux, or floats, that were sponsored by a collection of various organisations, as diverse as Young Farmers, The British Legion Woman's Section and the Royal Greenwich Observatory Sports Club. Before WW2 they tended to be pushed around on handcarts but after war progressed to tractors and other vehicles. These were towed around the town as part of the procession

Floats added to the colour and pageantry of the event

adding to the colour and pageantry of the event. All subjects were covered including, once, a complete Christmas party including turkey with all the trimmings and even a wrestling ring with two fighters who kept up the sport for three hours.

This tradition carried on well into the 1990s but as the event got more successful and the streets were crowded the logistics of towing large trailers on the back of tractors around a small town became impossible and BBB had to reluctantly ban tableaux from its processions.

In 1977 there was a new introduction to Battle bonfire celebrations called an effigy; in fact it was a modification of an old tradition. It was really a return to the BBB sponsored tableaux of the 19th and early 20th centuries. This was an

Very old picture not sure of age but would guess early 1930s
Along the top of the float it reads
"We'll all cling together to help the bonfire boys"
remember the 1930s was a bad time for the boyes

unexpected addition and when the crowd saw this first as a representation of Queen Elizabeth wheeled up the High Street, during her jubilee year, people were not quite sure what it was. Not realising the main purpose of the effigy, we the unsuspecting public, crowded around the Monarch which within minutes there was an exploding symphony of pyrotechnics and the good old public standing a mere few feet away. Health and safety! The creation was the work of local artist Max Blackman who legend has it, used to disappear for a few days and just turn up with the finished project. One day walking on the beat a local policeman came across a building which had a neon blue light and he thought "Hello, Hello, Hello what's going on here?" It was the Blackmans building the first effigy; "You're not suppose to know about this", was their reply to the inquisitive bobby. After explaining what it was, he told them their secret was safe with him. He didn't know it was full of fireworks.

Nobody really knew what the subject of the effigy was until the afternoon of the bonfire! Over the years his work included subjects as Batman, Ian Botham, Margaret Thatcher and even President Carter, which in itself caused political tension by the fact that American money had just bought Battle Abbey for The Department of Environment, which thought it was not in the best taste to lampoon an American. The Department of the Environment suggested that the BBB effigy should not be of politicians or members of the Royal Family, but would leave the final decision down to the Boyes. They took note of what was said and the following year the effigy was… Prince Charles.

Present effigy builder, Mark Oldroyd, who has been building since 1998, taking over from another local artist Robert Steormose, gives us an insight to the conception and building of the effigy. Ideas are buzzing around in his mind most of the year, but of course it has to be something the public remember in November so it has to be something reasonably current or something unforgettable. Once the idea has been conceived, building starts around the end of September. The building design has to be devised. Remember, its main purpose is to be a platform for the fireworks so that is the main consideration. The weather also needs to be taken into deliberations. There is no point if it blows over in the wind or gets soaked by a downpour. The main structure is wood and a union of hardboard and chicken wire. This is then covered with every child's favourite, papier-mâché constructed with a secret potion of glue and gum. After it has dried, the painting begins. Then

fireworks are added under the watchful eye of Mark protecting his newborn. Unlike Mr Blackman's approach, Mark likes the project to be finished a week or so before so that his only job on the day is to supervise the transportation to its final position. Mark recalled the first year he built the effigy he was not sure how big to build it. The advice was, as big as you like, unfortunately at nearly 20 feet high it took them over three and a half hours to go the one and half miles from its secret building location to its final firing position. Not forgetting that the structure had nearly thousand firework shells inside it as it inched its way through the town centre. When asked which effigy has been his personal favourite? Always the next one was his reply but the 2002 effort of Uncle Sam sitting on a bomb seemed to be high in his memory.

And how does he feel when his creation is destroyed by the fireworks? He finds it very satisfying that the town is eager to see his work as the fifth gets closer. Because there is always a "buzz" around town as to what the effigy will be.

His first priority is it has to good enough to be blown up as he sees it almost as a sacrifice to the Gods. Of course things do not always go to plan. The Darth Maul effigy which looked good on paper and looked good while it was lying down, but when it was stood up looked all out of proportion. So it was attacked with saws, given it a frontal lobotomy and a mere four feet out of his forehead. As with most creative people, Mark has strong views concerning censorship and interference from outside organisations, even as recently as 2004, which ironically, was a comment on free speech caused problems. Certain organisations were not happy with the wording, and it had to be altered at the last moment, and in fact at 9.30am on the day of the bonfire celebrations there was a doubt whether it would go ahead!

Unfortunately in these days of litigation the BBB have to be careful what is said or implied. This is not a new concept, as in 1951 the ESCC issued a mandate stating that effigies must be "Non Vulgar", otherwise their licenses will be "reviewed".

COMMUNITY SPIRIT

O f course the work of the Bonfire Boyes did not finish
after the clearing up of the bonfire remnants the next
day, or the following week in times past. Firstly there was
the important task of handing out the roadside collection, of
which every penny still goes to charity. Where the money
goes may have changed over the last hundred years but the
principle of small donations to a collection of causes still
stands. As seen before, the BHBB were an essential part of
the history of Battle Bonfire. They kept the celebration alive
at the turn of the 20th century and inaugurated two
additions to the celebrations that still exist to this day. The
1911 event included the innovative idea of a street
collection, which was in aid of the local hospital. The street
collection for charity is still the driving force behind today's
celebrations. All the monies raised on the street collections
have always and still go to charity. All the cost of staging the
bonfire is raised throughout the year, and not by collections
on the street. The BBB have never gone into handing out
large donations, their philosophy tends to be lots of little
ones, as the report from 1947 (on page 68) shows well.
Remember that this was only two years after WW2, and
people would still have been on food rations. Nothing short
of a marvellous effort.

The other innovative decision made by the BHBB when
they formed in 1907, was the then astounding decision to

The total distributed was £135, the same as last year, but the committee have approved of a further £10 from their own funds being held in trust as a grant towards the Battle Community centre.

It will be noted that the whole collected is distributed, nothing being retained either for expenses or the society funds. Since the war, £393 has so distributed.

Battle Nursing Association	£28 10s
Old Peoples (Christmas day) Treat	£20
Royal East Sussex Hospital	£20
Buchanan Hospital	£20
St Johns Ambulance (Battle)	£10
British Red Cross	£ 5 5s
Royal Lifeboat institution	£ 5 5s
Dr. Barnardo's	£ 3 3s
Battle Youth club	£ 3 3s
Battle Scouts	£ 3 3s
Battle Guides	£ 3 3s
Battle Ambulance	£ 2 10s
Old People (Battle charity)	£ 2 10s
Poppy Day	£ 2 2s
Police Orphanage	£ 2 2s
Royal Naval Benevolent Fund	£ 1 1s
Battle Army Cadet Welfare Fund	£ 1 1s
General Choir Fund (Battle Church)	£ 1 1s
St. Johns Ambulance Brigade Band	£ 1 1s

allow women into their procession.

Only in recent times has the BHBB been dropped from the full name of the society so maybe gone but the influence will never be forgotten.

All Bonfire Boyes who lived through earlier times come up with the same grumble. As with most things in the 21st century it has lost a bit of its community feel. Is that true or just as we get a bit older we see things differently? Battle Bonfire used to be a time when families get together a bit like Christmas. Families would return to their home town to enjoy the celebrations. Is that different today? I doubt it. The community spirit of the whole town would get involved with the celebrations. The base for the fifth's would be the local Butchers owned by Fred Holland which was mid way down the High Street. During the evening of the bonfire they would go into his cold room amongst the pigs and sides of beef, from there the operation would be

The decision to allow women into the procession when the BHBB
formed in 1907 was astounding for the time

controlled. Here they would have a few drinks and discuss the evening activities.

One year this local feeling showed itself as local chemist and great supporter of the bonfire Robert Emelues watched as a fellow Bonfire Boye who had been sampling the non meat menu in the butchers fell through his shop window. "Never mind I'll sort it out" was his reply. Would that happen now in today's litigious society? To add to the community spirit during his time, he and his wife would bring hot drinks and food to the Bonfire Boyes members around the bonfire later at night after most of the public had left for their beds.

A further community spirited activity was that on Christmas Day a number of Bonfire Boyes would go to the local Old People's hospital and help with the Christmas day dinner and sing a few carols for the patients. The BBB would also have made a donation towards the cost of the Christmas meal out of the street collection on the fifth. Are the modern day BBB any different? All the work is done voluntary. The street collections in 2005 raised a very respectable £5,500, all of which goes back into the community.

So is it still community based? Of course it is, just different as our community changes.

In the past the BBB held a Beef Pudding supper to finish the season as pictured below the table headed by the near legendary Mrs Hubbard the then owner of Battle Abbey and fanatical supporter of the Bonfire celebrations. As times change one of the last tasks now is the Battle Bonfire Inter Agency Meeting where all the groups involved review the event and its consequences. Were we all happy? Can it improve? Constant questions looking for answers.

The beef pudding supper to finish the season

BONFIRE NIGHT 2005

A PERSONAL VIEW OF THE 400TH CELEBRATIONS

The committee meetings have been going along for months as the organisation for such an event takes the best part of a year to arrange. One concern is that everyone is having their event on the fifth. This is a double edged sword as there will be lots of free advertising but the attendance will be a little smaller due to plenty of one off events for the 400th celebrations. There are fears that the procession will be very small as most other societies are being attracted to other celebrations. Other societies that usually support Battle bonfire are split as to where to go. This could have long term complications for the survival of Battle Bonfire and the smaller Bonfire celebration; let us hope this does not cause any long lasting grudges.

***

It is the end of October now; the meetings are now weekly. Different members appear at the meetings. Where have they been for the last six months? Also, the meetings are a little tenser as decisions are made and jobs have to be done.

Nov 3rd

A public chair has been placed and officially opened with a few words by Chairman Matt Southam on the Abbey Green in remembrance of all Battle Bonfire Boyes of the past. The most poignant being the memory of Paul Edmunds. Known to his friends as Badger, his family have been associated with the bonfire celebrations for many a year. His mother is current President of the society. The ceremony was closed with a short volley of fireworks.

Never have the words "Remember Remember" meant so much.

Nov 4th

The preparations for the celebrations of the "fifth" 2005 get moving in earnest today. A quick recognisance visit around the famous battlefield revealed that preparations for tomorrow's event were well under control. It is a unique setting for the 400th celebration of the attempt to remove the government of the day on the very field, where, 939 years earlier, the perpetrators of the same objective succeeded.

The simple but important job of erecting of the centre post for the affectionately known "Normus Gurt bonfire" is being prepared.

The delivery of the tubes for the fireworks and

positioning of the fences for the safety of the public were also set up in good time. We had to finalise agreement with English Heritage the idea of using the battlements for a unique view of tomorrow's events. They were extremely helpful offering us almost carte blanche access around the famous building, that is once we had sorted out the new contemporary tradition of public liability. We had to get a signature from the Chairman for our liability, so we rush off to the secret location where the effigy is being built. We are not permitted to enter the barn where the effigy is housed and had to wait outside like naughty school boys while a respected BBB went inside for the signature.

November 5th

7.00am

The town is deserted and sensible people are still asleep as the "Fifth" started bang on 7am with a volley of fireworks as an introduction to the ringing of the Church Bells, the first time this has happened in living memory. In times past the church bells use to ring at 5.00 am to welcome the town to the celebrations, in unison with a volley of the infamous Battle Rouser to wake the residents. This was usually a loud bang or six but the welcome in 1950 was certainly memorable for one early riser, when at 5.00 am the usual collection of Rousers were set off to signify the start of the bonfire day. They ran off down the street, one hit something, flew up into a bedroom window, landed in a chamber pot, exploded and sent the contents around the room.

A few fireworks are fired off on the Abbey Green as a reminder of things past. The fireworks seemed a bit reluctant to fire, let's hope that this is not a sign of things to come. It is as if to say, "It really is a bit early and we really should still be in bed."

7.20 am

It is our first trip of the day down to the battlefield. It is the main venue for tonight's bonfire and fireworks display. There is an eerie mist hanging over the valley which is covered with the first frost of the winter. With the ancient Abbey over looking the mist laden valley in ones mind we can almost here the battle cries of an ancient conflict drifting out of the silent dale. Away from the frost the ground is very wet, this may become a problem if it rains, as forecast, later today. No rain is the order of the day.

In fact there isn't a lot of action. A few guys are hanging around waiting for the first trailer of faggots to arrive. Amongst the flask of coffee and the early appearance of a few beer cans, there are tales of previous bonfire building adventures.

8.40am

At last the first load of faggots arrives. The tractor fights its way through the mud in the valley and climbs up through the mist like gifts from Mother Earth ready for the sacrifice. As it is the first load the BBB pounce on the load like (cliché warning) eager beavers to get the construction started. As in all groups of volunteers, as the hard work start, a few fade into the background or have other places to be. All too quickly these faggots are erected into position and the builders return to their pose around the tractor and trailer and their flasks of various liquids as if nothing had happened.

8.50am

The effigy arrives. Only a few elite members of BBB have seen it. There is an excitement in the air. It is very impressive, a selection of rockets all with the faces of the conspirators on. We were expecting a head of Guy Fawkes, we were surprisingly caught out and we admire the original

The drummers and children in fancy dress
provided an attention grabbing sight

*thinking of not just copying earlier ideas and just building
the head of dear old Guy Fawkes. It gets unilateral approval.
There is concern on faces as the Landrover and trailer starts
to slide on the wet hill, are we seconds away from disaster?
No the driver keeps it under control attacks the sea of mud in
the valley and to the relief of everybody arrives safely. Ten
minutes later, and with the help of everybody on site the
effigy has been lifted into position. There has been one
breakage as one of the rockets has fallen off its support, but
that is easily repairable.*

*An audible sigh of relief goes around the builders now that
the effigy is in its final resting place. There had been a slight
panic earlier, unbeknown to most, as there was a
miscalculation on the height of the effigy on the trailer and the
height of the building's door it was in. You can guess the rest.*

9.30am
The bonfire building had ground to a halt as there seems a

Constructing the bonfire

lack of faggots. So we walk up through the ruins of the Abbey back to the Green, our first visit since the reluctant fireworks which was over three hours ago. There has been a lot of activity taking place. The Bonfire Boyes have set up a merchandising table and the collection of badges and mugs are selling well, as always, all profits going into the fund to pay for the Bonfire Celebrations. We are waiting for the grand arrival of the pride and joy of BBB the "oldest Guy in the World". It is drawn through the High Street with great ceremony, accompanied by a noisy band of drummers and a group of young children in fancy dress. It is an attention-grabbing sight causing major traffic hold ups on a busy Saturday morning. The Guy takes its rightful centre stage position in the centre of the Abbey Green for all to see. With its striking features enhanced by the backdrop of the historic Abbey gatehouse and encircled by young smiling children in fancy dress with the bellowing sound of the drummers and the Church bells ringing it is really like we have travelled back to times past. We can not imagine the power the church had in the 17th and 18th century to keep the passion for this celebration. It is an irresistible attraction to the passer-by. As we wait on the green we watch two trailer loads of faggots being towed towards the battlefield. That will please the bonfire builders.

11.00am

Back to the battlefield and there is no sign of the two trailer loads of faggots! Where have they gone? How can it take over half an hour to travel the few hundred yards from the High Street? Has the spirit of Guy Fawkes wreaked a horrible revenge! Half an hour later the faggots arrive; there was a misunderstanding on who was going to open the gate. Over an hour has been lost. The construction restarts. Unlike some other Bonfire Societies it is not a matter of throwing branches on in a mass heap. It is an organised construction of to an aged old carefully conceived plan. Certainly there is a hierarchy as far as the building is concerned. The higher up

Getting everything ready

the hierarchy ladder is in proportion to how high up the bonfire you are allowed. Strangely it is all done in silence. I wanted to hear them singing Gospel songs as the fire was constructed. Within the hour there are faggots everywhere, what is the collective term for faggots, a bonfire of faggots maybe? Answers on a postcard please. There is just a very slight touchiness to the builders as they are about a couple of hours behind schedule. By now they are usually in a local hostelry partaking of another British tradition, the hearty, but unhealthy, English fried breakfast.

1.00pm

A little excitement as the first hotdog stands arrive. This is quickly followed by another food vendor. After a little discussion on where they were to set up they find a spot where everyone is happy. The owner should do as the Boyes ask why? It was 1957 when the first Hot Dog stand was allowed into the town. In his wisdom, the owner decided he did not want to donate to the Bonfire Boys collection boxes, even though he had done very well. Very soon there was an unscheduled "fireworks display" under his stand.

2.00pm

A quick word with the representative to English Heritage and they seem very happy. From their point of view everything is well under control. There is not much concern for the condition of the field which is getting a bit mangled. Any rain now and the conditions underfoot could get a little sticky. As we look out across the field, there are small groups of bonfire builders, fireworks' ground crew, effigy setters, all in a hive of activity. There is very little interaction between the groups almost as if they were trying to outdo each other in their importance.

Odd thing is while all this activity is going on the field is

The winners, and losers, of the guy
competition ready to be burned

still open to the visitors to the Abbey. They can walk around
everywhere including amongst thousands of pounds worth of
fireworks.

3.00pm
On the Abbey Green next to the merchandising tent there is
a Guy competition. These Guys will go on the small fire that
is being built on the Green. There are strict restrictions on
the size of this bonfire, including that it must be less than
eight feet high. The Boyes would not call this ideal but accept
it as a way of keeping the tradition of a fire on the Green
alive. The Guy making competition is thriving, with the
winners, and losers being banished to the flames on the small
bonfire later in the day.

3.30pm
We see Mr Chairman who says everything is behind schedule

but everything stops for tea. In fact they are stopping for lunch. But happily everything will be ready. Do the public realise how many people are involved with running this free event? BBB at present have a membership of around one hundred and fifty, of which a hardcore of about fifteen who do most of the setting up work during the year and as the event gets closer more get involved and on the day maybe fifty or sixty members and volunteers are involved with everything from marshalling to charity collections, setting off fireworks. In its height in the early 1950s, BBB had a membership of over two thousand to call on. Some members never actually get to see the show or the procession as they are all doing their bit, all doing it for nothing. Add to that, with all the emergency services and English Heritage, there must be 200 people involved in putting this together which costs the public nothing to witness. At 3.00pm we are all looking at the bank of black clouds approaching from the west hoping it won't deposit its contents and ruin everything.

6.00pm
The town is busy, but not at bursting point as it has been in the past. Maybe that is not a bad thing. The threat of rain seems to have dissipated. There is a fear for a low turn out, it is a difficult thing to predict on numbers because being the 400th celebration there are lots of alternatives and one off events. The weather is spookily mild for the time of year, almost saying "Go out and enjoy yourself". All the pubs and cafés are heaving.

6.15pm
Everything is ready to go. Thankfully no rain. The first entertainment for the night, Morris dancers, are out on the Abbey Green in front of the small bonfire entertaining the massing crowds. All dressed in black they get the evening off to a rousing start. This is followed by a spectacular display of

fire juggling which does give the evening that pseudo pagan feel which the crowd and participants are quite happy to go along with. It is interesting how over the last twenty years or so that various pagan ideals and imagery seem to be creeping into the celebration. This has not happened at any other time in its history. Is it another sign of how Christianity is falling from the masses?

7pm
Twelve hours into our day and now the town is buzzing. We were fortunate enough to have access to the roof of the Abbey Gatehouse for the best seats in the house. Climbing up the stone circular stairs winding up towards the roof, the cold still air in the stairwell smells of the brick and may have been there since it was built. From our vantage point on the Abbey Gatehouse we can see our first glimpse up the High

Operation room has police, ambulance and a security company all keeping a watchful eye on the event

The bonfire is ready to be lit

Street. We are away from the hustle and bustle in the town which gives our position an eerie calm. From the battlements the town looks packed. I can see for miles in the clear sky, with various fireworks going off on the edge of the town and beyond into Kent like the edges of a Catherine wheel with the centre point being Battle High Street. There is no boarding on the shops at all. This is the first time I can remember that and hope no one regrets not protecting their windows. There is a warm glow of anticipation radiating off the crowds.

7.30 pm
Behind the scenes the police and ambulances are meeting in the Abbey and there are about a dozen vehicles parked in

the Abbey courtyard out of sight, and after a quick briefing they disperse to various parts of the town. The operations room has police, ambulance and a security company all keeping a watchful eye on the event. It is all very calm all very well under control. In this modern day they have instant communications and camera watching everything.

7.45pm
There is a loud blast and the procession leaves a reputable few minutes late, I can just see it entering the top of the High Street, and there are still hundreds if not thousands of people filling the High Street. Where will they go? All of a sudden members of various services appear out of nowhere and join us on top of the Abbey for the best view of the events. The procession is led by a triad of police across the road and in front of them is Andrew Knowles-Baker with loudhailer to mouth as if Cecil B. de Mille moving his mass of extras ready to shoot the main scene behind him? In the wake of the parting people, in the front of procession being carried around regally ironically like a pope is the old guy. Unfortunately, the procession is a little modest in numbers but still noisy and upbeat. All the important people are there. Lewes is the most famous but can anything match the feel as the torched procession travels down the High Street up to the World Famous Gatehouse? This really is a secret that this part of Sussex knows about.

8.00pm
As the procession arrives at the bottom of the town a small group break away from the main group and on to the Abbey Green. They are not allowed into the Abbey any longer. In the days when the Abbey was privately owned, a delegation from the procession would enter the grounds, present themselves to the owners with a recital of the BBB chant and

The procession winds its way up to the bonfire

*return to the crowds depositing a volley of rousers while
passing through the gatehouse which would act like an
amplifier to create an ear shattering sound. The ancient
tradition of placing flowers in the bonfire is carried out.*

A few words are spoken by the Dean,

> *"We place flowers in this bonfire in thanks to God for the
> Bonfire Boyes in the past, who carried on this tradition in
> Battle. lets us pray that this fire and light shines out into
> the darkness tonight like God shines his light and his
> refined power into our lives making us holy to walk this
> life both in our town and our whole nation."*
> *Amen*

*The bonfire is lit by Mrs Rene Edmonds the Hon President a
few well organised fireworks are set off on the Abbey Green,
with banners in flares proclaiming the 400th celebrations. A*

great sight all set in front of Abbey accompanied by a small display of fireworks over the top of the Gatehouse. Maybe just one or two more than agreed but everyone seems happy.

8.30pm
The procession in its own time, winds its way around the traditional route up and down the High Street following in the footsteps of many a ghost of BBB and Rouser. It is hard work keeping the road clear for the procession to have a free run. In my view, considering where the bonfire and fireworks are now situated, the reasons for the trips up and down the High Street seem obscure, especially as most of the public move off the High Street and follow the procession to the bonfire site, on the first walk past. Of course I can understand the counter view that they do not want to see another tradition disappear.

9.00pm
The procession finds its way down on to the battlefield, there are a mass of 5000–6000 already waiting. The effigy looks very impressive under floodlights, there is a slight breeze. Perfect. The procession winds its way up to the bonfire which is sited on top of the hill in full view of the waiting crowds. A few words by the Chairman and another mass recital of the BBB chant the bonfire is officially lit by The Dean and then accompanied by a loud cheer and the presence of a mass of bangers and fireworks hundreds of torches are launched onto the fire. This was a little reluctant to take hold but eventually roared up in triumph.

Afterwards the Very Reverend Dr John Edmondson, the present Dean of Battle expressed the view that he is pleased to be involved with event as long as it remains a wholesome family occasion. He felt privileged to be asked to light the fire on its 400th celebration and was more than

Images of the procession from past and present

happy to arrange the Bells of the Church to rung in the morning as in days of olde. If there was any sign of anti-Catholic rhetoric returning, he feels he would have to reassess his position immediately. Of course, that is never going to happen, but he did express his fears over some Societies' use of burning crosses and other anti religious imagery. He would feel uncomfortable with his church being associated with the event if they were included in the procession.

It is strange how the image of burning crosses has found its way into the celebration. Was it someone's idea of what pagans do that caught on? Let us not forget the fact the celebration was born out of a win of Protestant Christians over Catholic Christians, so it is impossible to get away from the fact its foundations is a Christian celebration. It begs the question, if the Catholics were replaced today with another religion, would the event be allowed to go ahead?

Peculiarly up to the early part of the 20th century the fire was lit when the procession was around town.

9.30pm

After a bit of delay, while the last few spectators squeeze into the viewing area, the final and most spectacular part of the evening entertainment, the fireworks are about to get on their way. Starting with the original idea of two galleys representing the battle of Trafalgar exchanging volleys across the field, a superior, and noisy fireworks display followed – I cannot put that into words, look at the pictures! The finale was the effigy, which exploded in a barrage of light and sound for a mere ninety seconds but proved the best things do come in little spaces.

It was all over. Effigy builder Mark Oldyed, looks like a Saxon version of Winston Churchill with a huge cigar, relaxing in a proud satisfying afterglow of success.

10.30 pm

After the firework display the majority of the crowd drifts away, it's all over for another year and time now to relax.

Top: the superior and noisy firework display
Bottom left: The effigy rockets awaiting their fate
Bottom right: The ships representing the Battle of Trafalgar

The BBB dressed in their costume of choice with members of the procession were still around the fire enjoying the odd tipple and an unremitting salvo of bangers exploding. It is time for stories from around the fire.

AND FINALLY 401?

Four hundred years on and what of the future for Battle Bonfire and its Boyes? Where does it go in these days of million pound fireworks displays? There must be a place for these community based events in today's corporate calendars.

Throughout the history of the Bonfire Boyes it has always been a struggle to keep the event alive. To assist this The Bonfire Boyes as an organisation must realise that we are now in the 21st century before it is too late. If the event is to survive with television and other events on the very site that theirs is held they must have a plan as to where they wish to go. Just repeating the same formula as other events will not work. I commend them on the celebrations of 2005 with some new initiatives, but they must keep encouraging new ideas and new members.

More importantly Battle as a town must be fully behind it. A quick reminder that other events, even on the same venue have huge budgets and may seem more immediate, but their one and only goal is to make a profit. Let us not forget that the driving force behind the Bonfire is to raise money for charity, and the organisation has raised thousands of pounds for good causes during its lifetime.

Don't let it Die!

And I say a hearty well done and thank you to all Bonfire Boyes of today and days of olde:

Holla boys, holla boys, make the bells ring!
Holla boys, holla boys, God save the king!